Totally AMAZING MUMMIES

 A GOLDEN BOOK • NEW YORK

Golden Books Publishing Company, Inc., New York, New York 10106

Created by Two-Can for Golden Books Publishing Company, Inc. Copyright © 1998 Golden Books Publishing Company, Inc. All rights reserved.
Printed in the USA. No part of this book may be reproduced or copied in any form without written permission from the copyright owner.
GOLDEN BOOKS®, A GOLDEN BOOK®, TOTALLY AMAZING™, and G DESIGN™ are trademarks of
Golden Books Publishing Company, Inc. Library of Congress Catalog Card Number: 98-84147
ISBN: 0-307-20162-7   A MCMXCVIII

Amazing Mummies

Mummies are incredible dead bodies that have survived for thousands of years. All kinds of strange mummies—from people to pets—are found all over the world. Each mummy tells its own fascinating story about the past.

Believe it or Not

Scientists have discovered mummies of tiny animals, such as beetles and mice.

How Are Mummies Made?

The body of a mummy does not rot because it has been specially preserved. Sometimes bodies are mummified by accident, like when they are frozen in a block of ice. But usually a mummy has been preserved by an intricate process.

BOG WOMAN

DRIED-UP MAN

ICE MAN

Perfectly Pickled

The weather needs to be just right for bodies to be mummified naturally. In Egypt and China, the scorching desert heat has dried up bodies in the sand, while in Northern Europe a few mummies have been perfectly pickled in wet, marshy bogs.

Why Make Mummies?

Many ancient peoples believed that when a person died, he or she would start an exciting life in a strange new world. This was called the afterlife. It was thought that they would need their bodies in the other world, so they were made into mummies. The mummies were buried with food and drink and other home comforts for their new life.

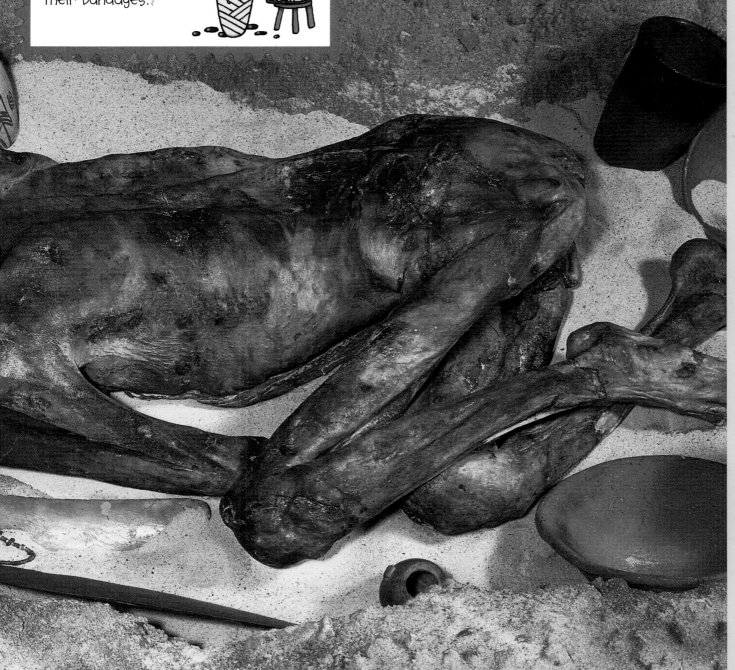

▲ At more than 5,000 years old, this mummy's a real old-timer. Discovered in a shallow sandy grave in the Egyptian desert, he was nicknamed Ginger because of the color of his hair.

HA HA! Why was the little Egyptian boy confused? Because his daddy was a mummy. HEE HEE!

Land of the Mummies

A GRAVE PLACE

Over 4,000 years ago, ancient Egypt became the world's number one mummy hot spot. This vast land was ruled by powerful kings called pharaohs. These kings wanted their bodies to be preserved forever. So people set to work to find a way...

Stop the Rot!

Before the ancient Egyptians started making mummies, all bodies were buried in sandpits. But powerful pharaohs didn't want to be treated in this way. They wanted tombs with lots of room. A lengthy process, called embalming, was perfected to make sure the mummy looked good for the afterlife.

▲ Ramses II ruled Egypt 3,000 years ago. His mummy is so well preserved that you can still tell what he looked like.

Pharaohs First

At first, only pharaohs were made into mummies, but soon the craze spread across the land. Rich people paid a fortune to become highly decorated mummies but the poor could only afford a basic makeover.

Mummy-makers

People who made mummies were called embalmers. They had a thankless job that involved treating the body and using special lotions to preserve the skin. Most Egyptians were mummified, so you can imagine how busy the embalmers were!

Cracking the Code

In 1798, the French emperor Napoleon led an expedition to Egypt. He brought scientists with him to study ancient Egyptian monuments, mummies' tombs, and a strange picture-writing, called hieroglyphs. No one could understand the hieroglyphs until an amazing discovery was made by accident!

One day, an officer in Napoleon's army found a stone at a place called Rosetta, near the Nile River. The stone was half-buried and covered in strange writing.

There were three kinds of writing on the stone, one of which was Greek. It took Jean-François Champollion, a French scholar, 23 years to figure out what it meant.

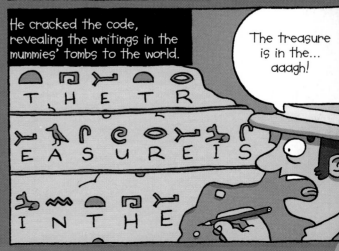

He cracked the code, revealing the writings in the mummies' tombs to the world.

The Underworld

The ancient Egyptians believed that when a person died, he had to travel through a hideous place that swarmed with fire-spitting demons. It was called the Underworld.

A DOOMED VACATION

It's judgment day and Anubis, the jackal-headed god, weighs the heart of the dead person against a feather, to see if the heart is heavy with sins. Thoth, who stands behind Anubis, records the verdic

Journey of Terror

A mummy needed help if it was going to survive the journey through the Underworld, so it was buried with a book which located hazards and listed useful spells. If the mummy made it to the end of its journey, its life was judged by 42 gods. If the mummy had behaved well, it went to a perfect place called the Field of Reeds. If not, it was eaten by a monster!

That's Weird

The ancient Egyptians couldn't wait to reach the Field of Reeds. Here the crops grew tall, there was lots of food, and everyone wore their finest clothes.

FIELD OF REEDS

So, no lunch again for me today.

Wrap and Roll

It took about 70 days to make a mummy and it was a smelly and messy job. As well as preserving and bandaging the body, embalmers recited spells to protect the mummy in the Underworld.

HOW TO MAKE A MUMMY

1 First cut open the body and take out all the internal organs, including the heart. Then pull out the brain through the nose.

2 Now wash the body with wine or vinegar. Pack natron salt around it and leave it to dry.

3 After 40 days, stuff the body with linen, leaves, or sawdust. Then put the heart back in and place glass eyes in the eye sockets.

amulet

4 Rub lots of oils and spices into the body, to stop the skin from drying and cracking.

5 Spend 15 days wrapping the body in bandages. Don't forget to slip a few charms in between the layers.

Strange but True

One mummy was wrapped in 3 miles (4.8 km) of bandages. That's enough to go around a football field 15 times!

Insides Out!

Are you wondering what happened to those internal organs left lying on the table? Well, they were stuffed into specially decorated pots, called canopic jars, and buried in the tomb with the mummy.

Mummy Makeover

As a finishing touch, the mummy's face was covered with a painted mask. Some masks showed what a person looked like before they died, but usually the mask was much more beautiful than the real face.

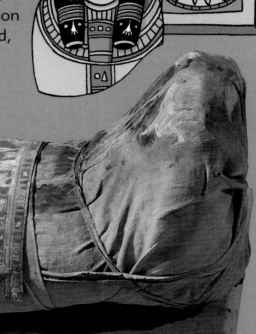

Here's a completely wrapped mummy. It's covered with a top wrapping called a shroud. An embalmer has placed an amulet, or charm, over the heart for good luck.

All Boxed Up

Painted cases for mummies were very popular with wealthy Egyptians. The mummies of poor Egyptians were either buried in a simple box, or put straight into the ground.

Safe and Sound

The first mummy cases were rectangular and long. They looked plain but were able to give a little protection against robbers who constantly tried to steal jewelry and charms from the mummy's body.

How many more to go?

All Shapes and Sizes

Later, mummy cases were given a new look and shaped with a head, shoulders, and feet. If you were rich, you could even be buried in lots of cases that fitted inside one another, just like Russian dolls.

Strange but True

Often, coffins were decorated with painted doors, so that the mummy's spirit could come and go when it felt like it!

Keeping a Look-out!

Usually, spells were painted on a case to keep the mummy safe. Some coffins even had spooky false eyes painted on, so that the mummy could see out. If anything terrible happened to the mummy, it was thought that the dead person's spirit could use the case as a spare body.

Who's watching who?

Cry-babies

When the case was closed, it was time to bury the mummy. Women were hired to cry and wail at the funerals of rich people. While the mummy was buried, mourners beat their chests, pulled their hair, and even flung soil over themselves.

▲ This mummy case belongs to a priestess called Shepenmut. A goddess spreads her wings across the case, protecting the mummy inside.

Pet Mummies

The ancient Egyptians didn't only make people into mummies—they wrapped up their pets too. There was room for millions of happy animals in the afterlife.

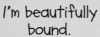

I'm beautifully bound.

Beastly Disguise

All kinds of creatures were bandaged up—fish, birds, and even snakes! They were made into mummies because the ancient Egyptians thought that many animals were really gods in disguise.

Help! I can't get out.

Sticky Business

A few unlucky creatures ended up as mummies by accident. Flies came to a sticky end by falling into a hot resin that was poured over the mummy's body. And small lizards were sometimes trapped between the bandages.

Holy Cow!

One special bull, called the Apis, was thought to be sacred. This bull lived a life of total luxury—he even had servants! When the bull died, it was mummified and buried in a style fit for a pharaoh. It had a stone coffin, called a sarcophagus, that weighed more than a truck.

That's Weird

Even ferocious crocodiles were made into mummies. These were sacred reptiles that lived at the temples. Visitors fed them meat and wine and dressed them in expensive gold jewelry!

The Case for Cats

The ancient Egyptians were crazy about cats. When pet cats died, their owners became so upset that they shaved off their own eyebrows. Then they mummified the cats and buried them in cat-shaped cases, so that they would see them again in the afterlife.

Cat Crime

It wasn't a clever idea to bug an ancient Egyptian cat. The Egyptians believed that cats were sacred and if anyone was caught harming one, he or she could be sentenced to death. The cats that lived around temples were particularly lucky. People brought food and milk to honor the fortunate felines.

I'm purrfectly wrapped!

▲ Cat mummies were often given expressions. This one is smiling.

13

Pyramid Power..
...Homes for Old Bones

The pharaohs made sure that they had everything they needed for their luxurious lives in the next world. When they died, they were buried in spectacular tombs, called pyramids, packed full of goodies.

Take-away Treasure
The first pharaohs had their mummies buried deep inside pyramids in chambers filled with gold, jewels, and other treasures. There were also useful items such as clothes, food, and furniture. And for rainy days in the Field of Reeds, there were even games!

Believe it or Not

The Great Pyramid at Giza is the largest human-made building in the world.

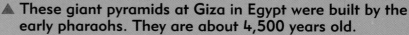

These giant pyramids at Giza in Egypt were built by the early pharaohs. They are about 4,500 years old.

That's Weird

The Egyptians believed that the sloping sides of a pyramid represented the slanting rays of the sun. The spirit of a pharaoh used the rays to climb up to heaven.

A few of the early pharaohs had a gruesome solution to taking it easy in the next world. They had their servants killed and buried with them!

Later, pharaohs were buried with hundreds of small model servants, called shabtis. These models were thought to magically spring to life in the afterlife, and slave away for their lazy masters.

Tomb Raiders

Every Egyptian, including robbers, knew that the pyramids were piled high with tempting treasures. The pharaohs tried to make their pyramids burglar-proof, but they didn't succeed.

PYRAMID PESTS

Treasure Trail

The Book of Buried Pearls was a step-by-step guide to tomb raiding. It gave would-be looters lists of hidden hoards, maps showing where to find the goodies, and spells to outwit the guardian spirits inside the tombs.

Off With Their Heads!

The tomb robbers were often the workers who had helped to build the tombs in the first place. With a little help, they could find the treasure, sell it, and look forward to a life of luxury. But if they were caught, they were tortured and executed.

Get your death mask here.

TRICKING THIEVES

That'll fool them.

Pyramid builders tried to fool thieves by sealing the entrance with a mighty slab of stone.

If robbers got in, then they had to find their way through a maze of tunnels, dead ends, and deep wells.

Aaaaaaaargh!

I'm almost there!

Robbers chipped away at the walls. Just when they thought they'd found the treasure ... a huge stone blocked the way!

End of the Pyramids

Eventually, the pharaohs became so fed up with pyramid-plundering, that they changed their tactics. Instead of building pyramids, they had their mummies and their possessions buried in secret tombs, cut into the cliffs of a desert valley called the Valley of the Kings. But soon the thieves caught on and the looting began again.

Mummy Medicine

Treasure was not the only reason for tomb raiding. Mummies had their uses, too. In 17th-century England, people thought that powdered mummy was a magical healing potion. They rubbed it into their skin or swallowed it as a medicine.

Full Steam Ahead!

Mummies were also used as fuel, because the oils and resins on their wrappings burned well. Up until about 70 years ago, Egyptian trains ran on fuel made from thousands of burning mummies.

▲ Tomb raiders left behind this mummified head. It was discovered in one of the looted tombs in the Valley of the Kings.

The World's Most Famous Mummy

At a Snail's Pace

Howard Carter was a real slowpoke. He spent ten years searching for the tomb. Then he took eight years to clear out over 5,000 objects and another ten years to list them all in detail. Carter was so thorough and patient that he didn't even open the first coffin until almost three years after he had found it!

The thieves made off with lots of loot, but they missed the star prize—the tomb of King Tutankhamen. When this hideaway was discovered by Howard Carter in 1922, it had not been opened for 3,000 years.

Zzzzzzzzz.

Golden Goodies

Inside the tomb, there were piles of golden objects, including necklaces, bracelets, thrones, chariots, tables, statues, swords, and shields. There were also about 100 pairs of shoes, 30 boomerangs, ostrich feather fans, trumpets, and a first-aid kit.

98...99...

The King's Case

Tutankhamen was a young pharaoh who died when he was about 20 years old. He was buried inside three beautiful, decorated cases, which fitted snugly one inside another. The smallest case was made of solid gold.

Behind the Mask

Tutankhamen's mummy wore a glittering gold mask, studded with semi-precious stones. It weighed more than 22 pounds (10 kg). The mask was so firmly stuck to Tutankhamen's head that scientists had to slide hot knives underneath it to pry it off.

Strange but True

Tutankhamen collected earrings. Inside his tomb, there were several pairs to wear in the afterlife.

△ This is the second of Tut's three classy cases. But the face on this case is different from the others. Was it made for someone else?

The Mummy's Curse

There seemed to be a price to pay for disturbing Tutankhamen. Several people connected with the discovery of the tomb died soon afterwards. Rumors spread that they were victims of a 3,000-year-old curse...

Lordy, Lordy

Lord Carnarvon was victim number one. Five months after entering Tut's tomb, he died from a mosquito bite on his cheek. At the moment of his death, all the lights in Cairo went out. Back in England, his dog let out a howl and dropped dead.

Get Carter

If there was a curse, Howard Carter should have been first in line for a visit from the grave. After all, he'd been the one to break into Tut's tomb! But he dismissed reports of the curse as "ridiculous stories." He lived on for many more years, until his death in March 1939—from natural causes.

Mummies in the Movies

A curse makes for a great story and Hollywood loved the idea of a mummy wreaking revenge from beyond the grave. In 1932, Boris Karloff starred in *The Mummy*, the first in a long line of horror movies featuring bandaged zombies. Karloff based his grizzly, tattered looks on a real mummy of an ancient Egyptian pharaoh, Tuthmosis III.

That's Weird

On the day that Tut's tomb was opened, Carter's pet canary was gobbled up by a giant cobra. Big deal, huh—except that Tut's mummy mask has a cobra on its forehead!

Mummies became the spooky inspiration for many films made in Hollywood during the 1930s and 1940s.

Bog Mummies

Across Northern Europe, nearly 2,000 ancient bodies have been plucked from murky peat bogs and marshes. Some of the bodies are so well-preserved that archaeologists can even take their fingerprints.

How did I end up lying here?

Mistaken Identity

In 1952, gruesome Grauballe Man was found in a bog in Denmark. Local people thought he had toppled into the bog 70 years previously after a rowdy night out. Later they discovered he was 1,500 years old.

Believe it or Not

Most mummies are red-heads. Acids in the soil and sand make the hair on most mummies turn red.

▲ Grauballe Man ate his supper before he fell into his watery grave. The scientists who examined his body discovered wheat, rye, and weed seeds swimming around inside his stomach. Mmm, tasty!

A Deep Sleep

The circumstances surrounding Tollund Man's death were more suspicious. This 2,000-year-old sleeping beauty was found in a bleak bog in Denmark with a leather noose around his neck. Archaeologists think that Tollund Man was probably hanged as a sacrifice to the gods.

Hey, great tan!

Getting a Tan

When Lindow Man was hauled out of a moist peat bog in England in 1984, he looked like he had spent far too long on a sun-drenched beach in the Bahamas. Acid in the peat had given him an all-over tan and turned his skin to leather.

Manicured Mummy

Archaeologists carefully studied Lindow Man for clues to his identity. They worked out that he was about 25 years old when he died. His hands were smooth and his fingernails were neat which meant that he hadn't done much manual work. Maybe he was a chief?

Ice Mummies

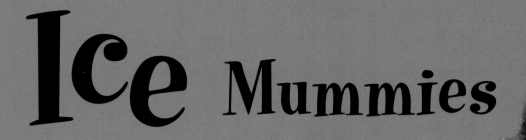

If you're planning on making a mummy, take a swift trip to icy lands in the north of the world. There, you can freeze-dry a body in the chilly air or make your own human popsicle in a block of ice.

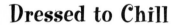

Dressed to Chill

This mummy of a tiny Inuit boy was buried in the snow in Greenland. His relatives decked him out in a cozy fur parka, thick trousers, and padded boots to keep out the bitter cold as he trekked into the next world.

Believe it or Not
Once, a freeze-dried chicken was discovered behind the walls of a house in England.

THE ICEMAN

Around 3,000 BC, a traveler was hiking through a snowy mountain pass high in the Alps in Italy.

I'll just take a quick nap.

Suddenly a storm blew up. He sheltered under a rocky overhang. The traveler lay down to rest as the storm raged on.

But the man never woke up. His body was frozen. It was covered in snow for 5,000 years until two hikers found him in 1991.

Let's call him Iceman.

Mummies in the Freezer

In 1993, archaeologists in Russia unearthed a magnificent tomb from the bleak, windswept lands of Siberia. It belonged to the ancient Pazyryk people and was hidden far below the ground. Rainwater had seeped into the tomb and turned it into a giant deep freezer.

mummified horses

stone cover

man in shallow coffin

log chamber

woman in carved coffin

food and drink for the afterlife

All Dressed-up

Inside there was a scene frozen in time—everything was perfectly preserved. A Siberian man rested in a shallow coffin on the roof, while an important woman slept below. She was swathed in luxurious furs and wore a wooden headdress carved with cats and swans and covered in gold. On her shoulders and wrists, there were tattoos of wondrous beasts.

Tell Me Why

ICE MUMMIES TRY TO KEEP COOL

Ice mummies hate warm weather! When their frozen bodies are taken from their chilly tombs, they soon begin to melt. Within a few days, the warm temperatures make a creeping, smelly fungus grow on the mummies!

ICE CREAM

FROZEN PIZZA

MUMMIES

Scientists store mummies in giant refrigerators to keep them fresh. The mummies are taken out only on special occasions, and then just for short periods.

Odd-ball
Mummies

Mummies turn up all over the place. Each one has its own unique style, from a well-dressed body lying in a coffin to a seated corpse in a cloth bundle.

Mystery Man of China

One mummy discovery gave archaeologists a real headache. Determined investigators uncovered an ancient tomb in China, but the three bodies inside it, including the man above, were not Chinese. Instead, they came from a tribe from Europe. No one knows how they ended up in China.

That's Weird

In Japan, mummy-makers preserved dead priests by lighting huge candles and smoking the bodies dry!

Toasty!

Dead-heads

In the past, the Chimu people of Peru gave their dead false heads. When family members died, they were hung out in the sun to dry. Then, relatives squashed them into a cloth bundle and made them fake heads. Wigs of human hair, shell eyes, and feather eyelashes were added as a final touch.

Nice eyelashes!

A Date with the Dead

Did you know that a few people used to have lunch with mummies? In Italy, around 6,000 mummies are stored in an underground tomb. Their living relatives used to bring picnics to the tomb and chat to the mummies, as though they were alive.

Pass the pizza.

Ruling Bodies

When a ruler of the ancient South American Inca people died, his subjects dried his body in the cool mountain air. They treated the mummy as though it were still their leader, and brought it food and drink every day. They even took it on day trips to visit other mummies!

How To Get a Head!

The Jivaro Indians in South America used to chop off an enemy's head and plop it in boiling hot water to make it shrink, just like a wool sweater. Then they stuffed the shrunken head with hot sand and wore it around their necks at special festivals. They believed it would give them the dead person's strength.

Two heads are better than one!

Mummy Detectives

Being a mummy detective is a gruesome but great job. Scientists study mummies to find out how people lived long ago, what clothes they wore, and even how they died.

Strange but True

The mummy of Ramses II has an extremely long second toe, which is typical of an ancient Egyptian foot.

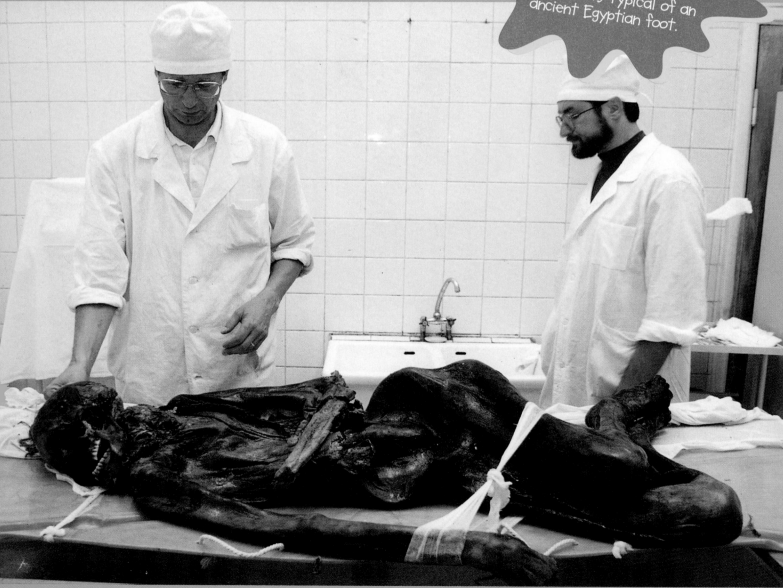

▲ This mangled mummy was a Siberian warrior. By looking at his skin and bones, scientists can figure out the kinds of injuries he suffered in battle.

That's Weird

In England in the 1800s, a mummy unwrapping was a crowd-drawing event. Surgeons carried out the honors before an amazed audience, sometimes using a hammer and chisel to remove the hardened bandages.

Open Wide!

A mummy's mouth can tell you a lot. By looking at a mummy's teeth, you can tell how old a person was when he or she died. You can also find out a mummy's favorite meal. Worn teeth show that the mummy's daily bread was full of sand and grit!

Tools of the Trade

Scientists also take samples of skin and bone from mummies. They can tell if the person had any germs or diseases when he or she was alive. And with X-ray machines, scientists can take pictures of a mummy's insides. By studying the contents of a mummy's stomach, they can reveal what the mummy ate for a last supper.

Tell Me Why

RAMSES II NEEDED A PASSPORT

In 1974, horrified scientists discovered that the mummy of the pharaoh Ramses II had a weird skin infection. The mummy was flown to Paris for tests. He was given a passport which listed his job as "King (deceased)"!

Luckily, scientists in Paris were able to cure him quickly. While examining his body, they also learned that the clever Egyptian embalmers had stuffed Ramses' nose with peppercorns to keep its hooked shape.

Mummy Museum

Welcome to the spookiest museum of them all! Many of the top mummies, from the loveliest to the oldest, are packed into these pages.

Fishy Tale

Mummies don't come any stranger than this. One man tried to trick the world into believing that he had found a mummified merman—the half-man, half-fish creature from old sea legends. He took the head of a monkey and tail of a fish and joined them together to make a mummy.

Are you for real?

Loveliest Lady

This lady, nicknamed the Loulan Beauty, wins the beauty contest for mummies. When she was found in China in 1980, she became famous for her lovely face and long hair. Artists have even painted pictures of how they think she looked before she died.

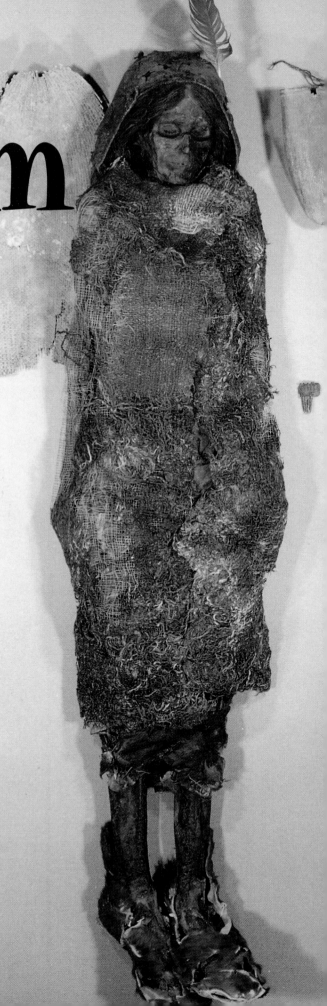

King of Cool

Hello Gramps.

The coolest mummy must be the Iceman. He's so ancient that he had already been frozen for almost 1,000 years when the ancient Egyptian pharaohs were being buried. Old Iceman still looks pretty good for his age!

Waxy Wonder

One of the most popular mummies is the Russian leader, Vladimir Lenin. His eerily life-like body was mummified in 1924, using a top-secret wax process. Since then, he's had thousands of visitors every day.

True or Fake?

In AD 79, a volcano in Italy erupted near the town of Pompeii, burying alive over 2,000 ancient Romans under a layer of hot ash.

The dead bodies rotted away, leaving behind hollows in the hardened ash. Recently, archaeologists poured liquid plaster into the hollows, making mummy-like copies of the dead.

Mountain Maiden

This Inca girl is the tops! Her mummified body was found an incredible 20,700 feet (6,313 m) up, on top of a volcano in the Andes Mountains of South America. Experts believe she was put there as a gift to the mountain gods.

Index and Glossary

Illustrations: Andrew Peters
Consultant: Del Pemberton
Author: Iqbal Hussain
Photographs: Cover: Science Photo Library; p1: Science Photo Library; p3: The British Museum; p4: Sygma; p6/7: The British Museum; p8/9: The British Museum; p9 (top): The British Museum; p10: The British Museum; p11: Royal Albert Memorial Museum, Exeter/Bridgeman Art Library; p12: The British Museum; p13: The British Museum; p14/15: The Stock Market; p17: The Egyptian Museum, Turin, Italy/ Werner Forman Archive; p18/19: Robert Harding Picture Library; p19 (top): Robert Harding Picture Library; p21: Advertising Archives; p22/23: Moesgard Museum; p23 (top): Science Photo Library; p24: Greenland National Museum and Archives; p26: Sygma; p27: National Geographic Society; p28: Sygma; p30: Sygma; p31: Rex Features.